WEIRD SCIENCE

MEDICINE

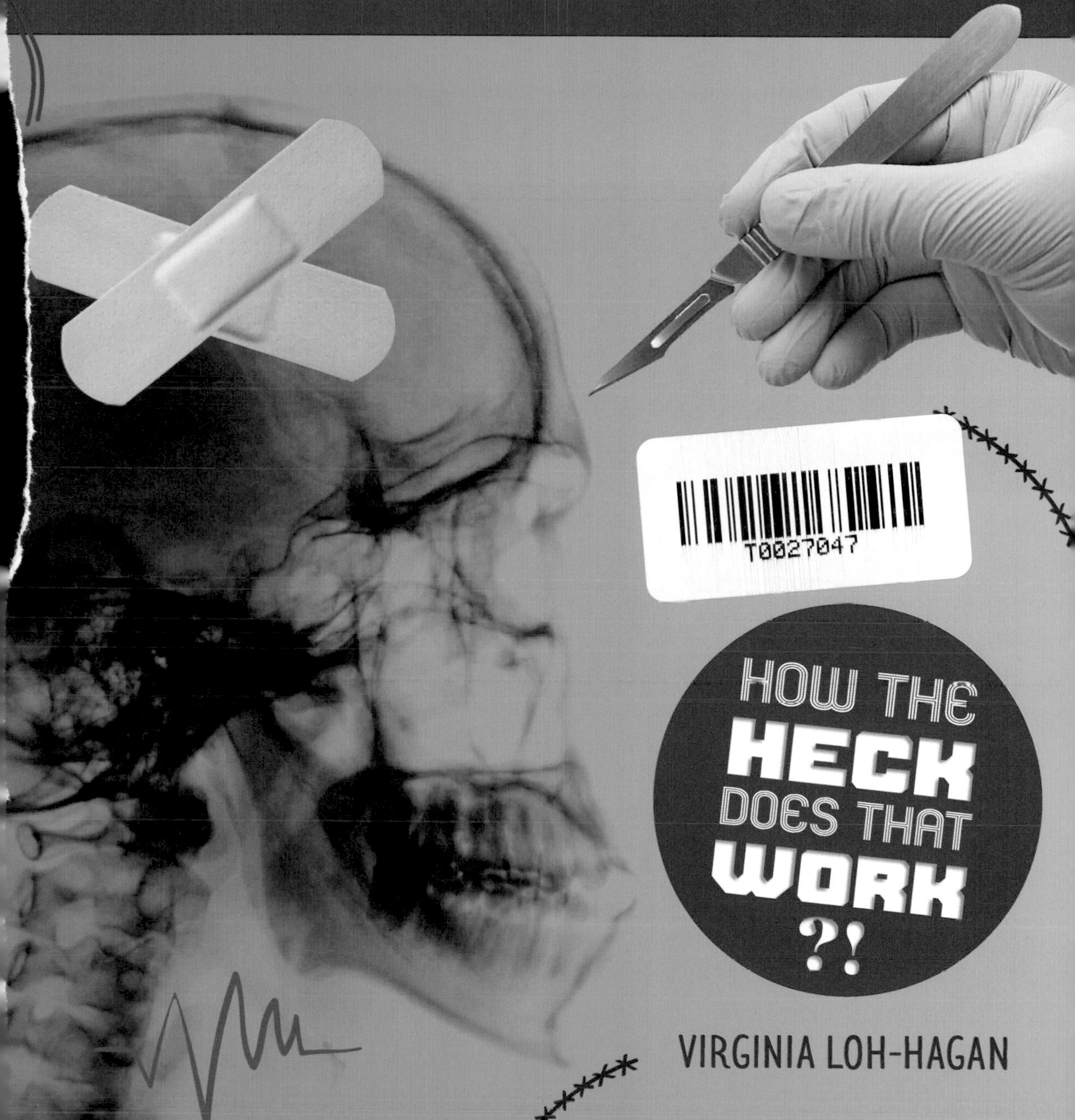

HOW THE **HECK** DOES THAT **WORK** ?!

VIRGINIA LOH-HAGAN

45TH PARALLEL PRESS

Published in the United States of America by Cherry Lake Publishing Group
Ann Arbor, Michigan
www.cherrylakepublishing.com

Reading Adviser: Beth Walker Gambro, MS, Ed., Reading Consultant, Yorkville, IL
Book Designer: Felicia Macheske

Photo Credits: © Puwadol Jaturawutthichai/Shutterstock, cover, 1; © Netkoff, cover, 1; © 168 STUDIO/Shutterstock, cover, 1; © S_Kuzmin/Shutterstock, cover, back cover, 1, 3; © Stock Up/Shutterstock, back cover; © Channarong Pherngjanda/Shutterstock, back cover, 5; © Africa Studio/Shutterstock, back cover, 31; © Sean Locke Photography/Shutterstock, 4; © Julio Ricco/Shutterstock, 6; © DC Studio/Shutterstock, 7; © Chinnapong/Shutterstock, 8; © Tasha Drik/Shutterstock, 9; © Science History Images / Alamy Stock Photo, 10; © EDSON DE SOUZA NASCIMENTO/Shutterstock, 11; © leopictures/Shutterstock, 12; © Morphart Creation/Shutterstock, 13; © Yurii Andreichyn/Shutterstock, 14; © Radharc Images / Alamy Stock Photo, 15; © plenoy m/Shutterstock, 16; © Lothar Drechsel/Shutterstock, 18; © Barashkova Natalia/Shutterstock, 19; © Buntoon Rodseng/Shutterstock, 19; © Mark_Kostich/Shutterstock, 20; © Drawlab19/Shutterstock, 22; © Pictorial Press Ltd / Alamy Stock Photo, 23; © Luuuusa/Shutterstock, 24;© Fine Art Studio/Shutterstock, 26; © CkyBe/Shutterstock, 26; © dpa picture alliance archive / Alamy Stock Photo, 27; © Photographee.eu/Shutterstock, 28; © INTERFOTO / Alamy Stock Photo, 30;

45th Parallel Press is an imprint of Cherry Lake Publishing Group.

Library of Congress Cataloging-in-Publication Data

Names: Loh-Hagan, Virginia, author.
Title: Weird science : medicine / by Virginia Loh-Hagan.
Description: Ann Arbor, Michigan : Cherry Lake Publishing, 2021.
| Series: How the heck does that work?! | Includes index.
Identifiers: LCCN 2021004919 (print) | LCCN 2021004920 (ebook)
| ISBN 9781534187603 (hardcover) | ISBN 9781534189003 (paperback)
| ISBN 9781534190405 (pdf) | ISBN 9781534191808 (ebook)
Subjects: LCSH: Medicine—Juvenile literature.
Classification: LCC R130.5 .L64 2021 (print) | LCC R130.5 (ebook) | DDC 610—dc23
LC record available at https://lccn.loc.gov/2021004919
LC ebook record available at https://lccn.loc.gov/2021004920

Cherry Lake Publishing Group would like to acknowledge the work of the Partnership for 21st Century Learning, a Network of Battelle for Kids. Please visit *http://www.battelleforkids.org/networks/p21* for more information.

Printed in the United States of America
Corporate Graphics

Dr. Virginia Loh-Hagan is an author, university professor, and former classroom teacher. She's currently the Director of the Asian Pacific Islander Desi American Resource Center at San Diego State University. She dedicates this book to the doctors, nurses, and hospital workers who supported patients during the COVID pandemic. She lives in San Diego with her very tall husband and very naughty dogs.

TABLE OF CONTENTS

Many people work in the medical field. There are doctors, nurses, scientists, hospital workers, and more.

INTRODUCTION

All kinds of weird science happen in medicine. When something happens to our bodies, doctors help. Doctors use medical science. Medical science tries to explain how the body works. Scientists work in medical science. They perform tests to detect sicknesses. They find ways to prevent and treat sicknesses.

Margaret Mead was a scientist in the mid-1900s. She studied human history. She said a healed bone was the first proof of civilization. This bone was 15,000 years old. Mead said people with broken bones would die. A healed bone meant someone cared for that person. This caring is what makes humans more advanced than animals.

Medical scientists care about human lives. They heal people. They keep people alive. They keep people healthy. They solve problems. They create tools. They do research. They study human bodies. They're always learning.

Medical science keeps improving. Scientists make better tools. They make better medical drugs. Drugs are used to cure sicknesses. Today, people have longer lifespans. They survive sicknesses. They have healthier and happier lives. Medical science saves lives.

Dare to learn more about medical science! So much is going on. How the heck does it all work?

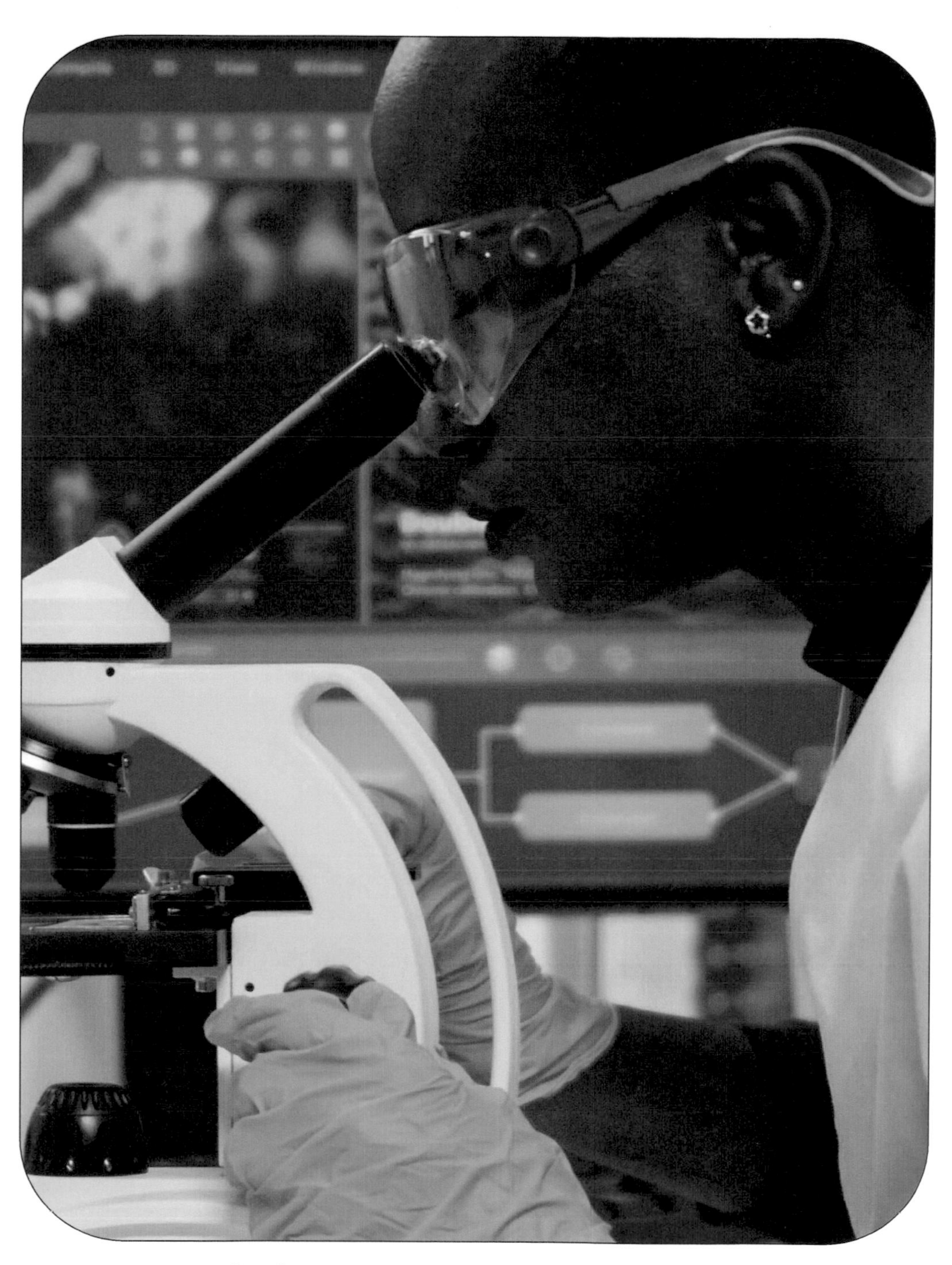

Many medical scientists work in a labs.

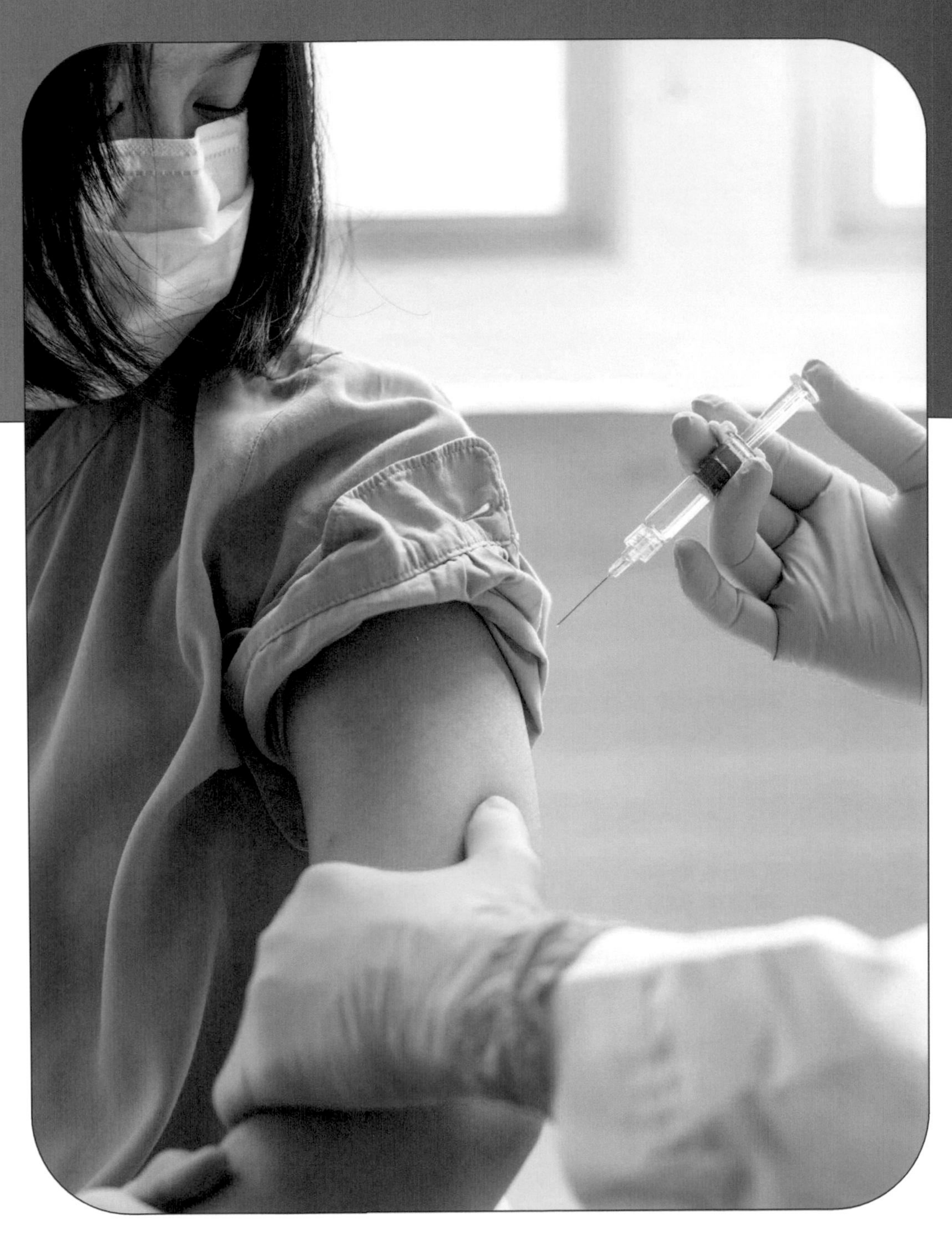

Vaccines trigger an immune response.

CHAPTER 1

VACCINES

Have you ever been sick? Chances are germs are to blame. Germs are everywhere. But your body can defend itself. When germs enter your body, this sets off your **immune** systems. Immune means resisting sicknesses. The germs are destroyed. But some germs are too strong. That's why **vaccines** exist. Vaccines can protect people against **diseases**. Diseases are serious sicknesses.

Most vaccines contain dead or weak germs of a disease. These germs are injected into people. Vaccines help immune systems recognize germs. They make **antibodies** that will attack germs in the future. Antibodies are produced by cells in the body that fight off sicknesses.

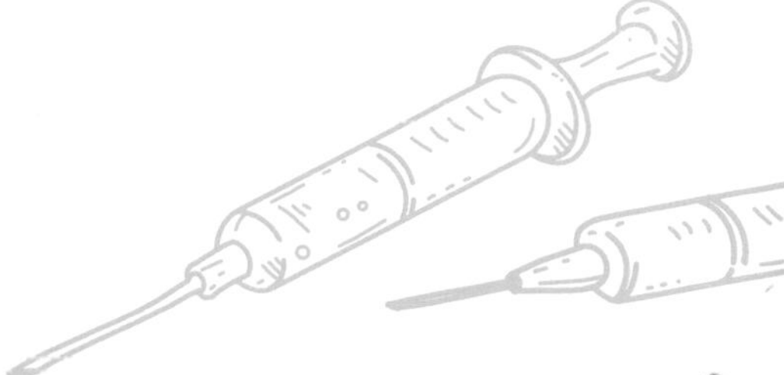

The first vaccine was developed in the late 1700s.

Some vaccines need to be injected more than once. This allows immune systems to develop memory cells. This helps your body train to fight the disease.

Once enough people get vaccines, disease **outbreaks** are low. Outbreaks happen when a lot of people get sick. With vaccines, germs won't have enough **hosts**. Hosts are people who carry disease germs. Vaccines stop germs from spreading. Germs will die out. This is called **herd immunity**.

Herd immunity helps people who can't get vaccines. Vaccines may not be safe for babies, older people, and others. Some people are allergic to vaccines. Some people are too sick for vaccines.

Vaccines have nearly wiped out some diseases. Examples are polio and mumps.

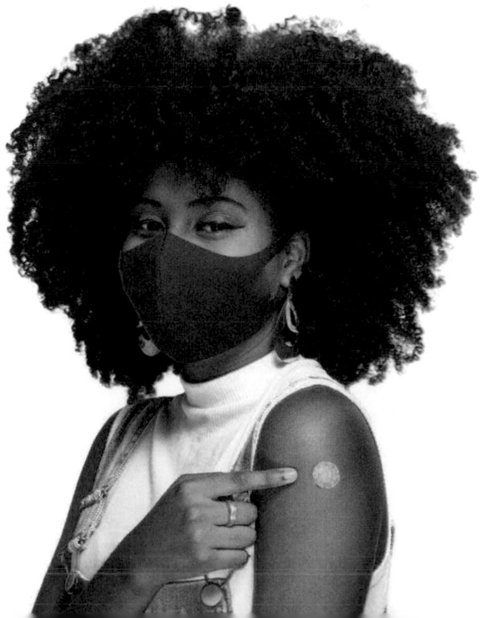

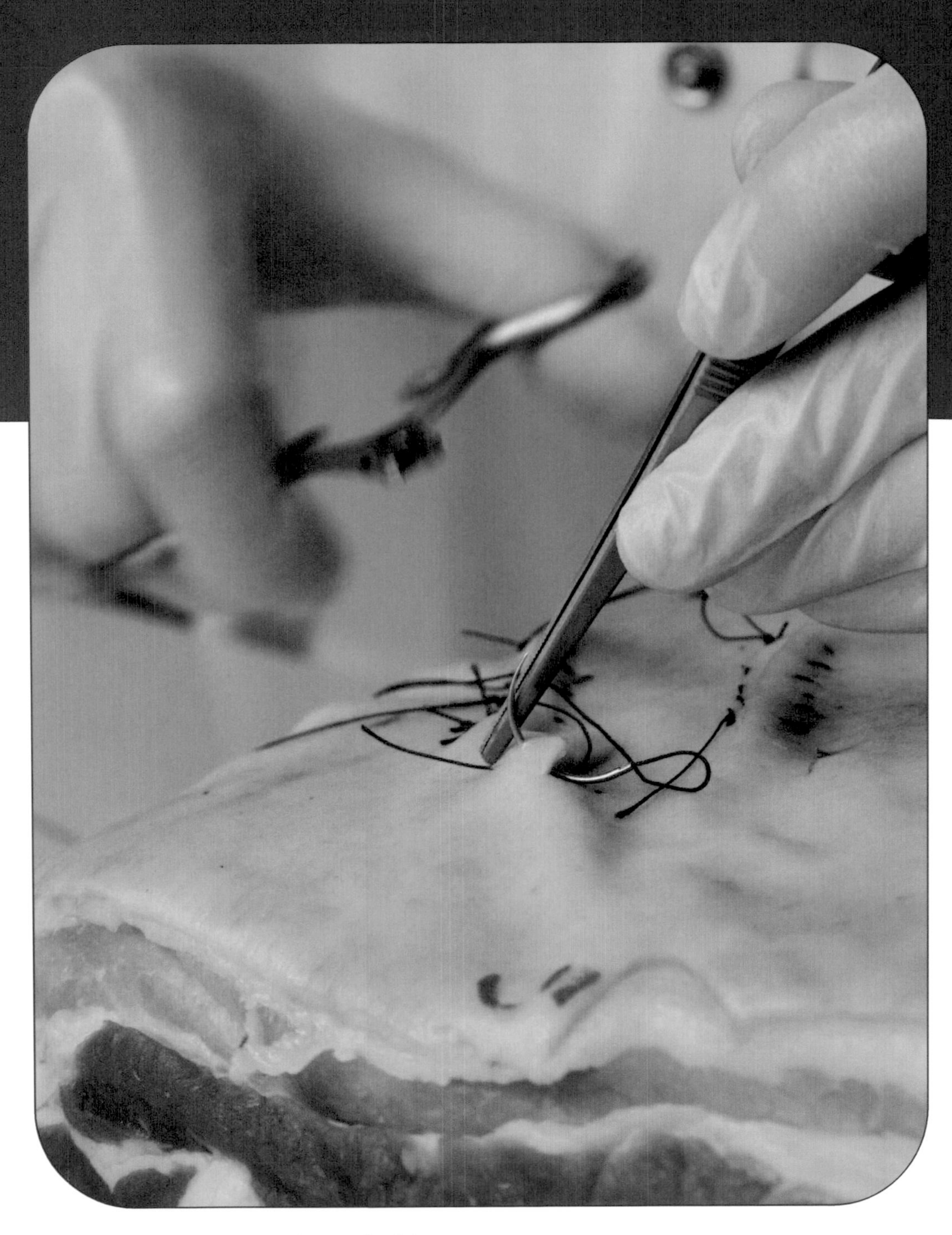

Doctors practice stitching on grapes and chicken meat.

CHAPTER 2

STITCHES

What do you do when you have a cut? Most cuts heal on their own. But some cuts are too deep. They're open wounds. This means germs and dirt can get in. This can cause infections. Infections can make people sick. Deep cuts need stitches.

Doctors must clean the cut. They remove the dirt. They remove dead cells. Then, they use medicine to **numb** the area. Numb means to feel no pain. Doctors pull the skin edges together. They sew the wound closed with stitches. Closing the wound gives the area time to heal. Skin and other cells regrow. They join together. When the healing is done, doctors remove the stitches.

Even WEIRDER MEDICAL SCIENCE!

- Doctor fish are in the Middle East. They're used to treat skin issues. People with itchy, flaky skin go to a hot spa. They get into a pool. Doctor fish swim around their bodies. They eat the skin flakes. They relax people.

- Medical scopes are long tubes. They're flexible. They have a light. They're put inside bodies. They let doctors see what's happening inside. They need to be cleaned very well to not spread germs. But these tools are hard to clean. Scientists are working on making disposable scopes. Disposable is something that can be thrown away.

- Doctors are now using 3-D printers. 3-D means three-dimensional. It means not flat. These printers make things that look real. They're used in medicine to make replacement limbs. Limbs are arms and legs. These special printers could also be used to make replacement organs. Organs are groups of tissues. Tissues are the materials that form parts of your body. They have a specific job. Scientists are working on making replacement organs. This process is called bio-printing. Scientists make organs that grow in people's bodies. The printed organs replace the damaged ones.

For some stitches, doctors use special thread. This thread **dissolves** over time. Dissolves means to melt away.

Bodies see stitches as foreign. They're designed to attack anything foreign. Some dissolvable stitches are natural. They're made from animal guts. Or they're made from silk and hair. They're made from other natural products. All dissolvable stitches **decompose** in the body. Decompose means to break down. They dissolve when wounds are healed.

Dissolvable stitches are strong in the beginning. They're made of many fibers. They won't break. They lose their strength over time. Bodies can dissolve them from a few days to several months.

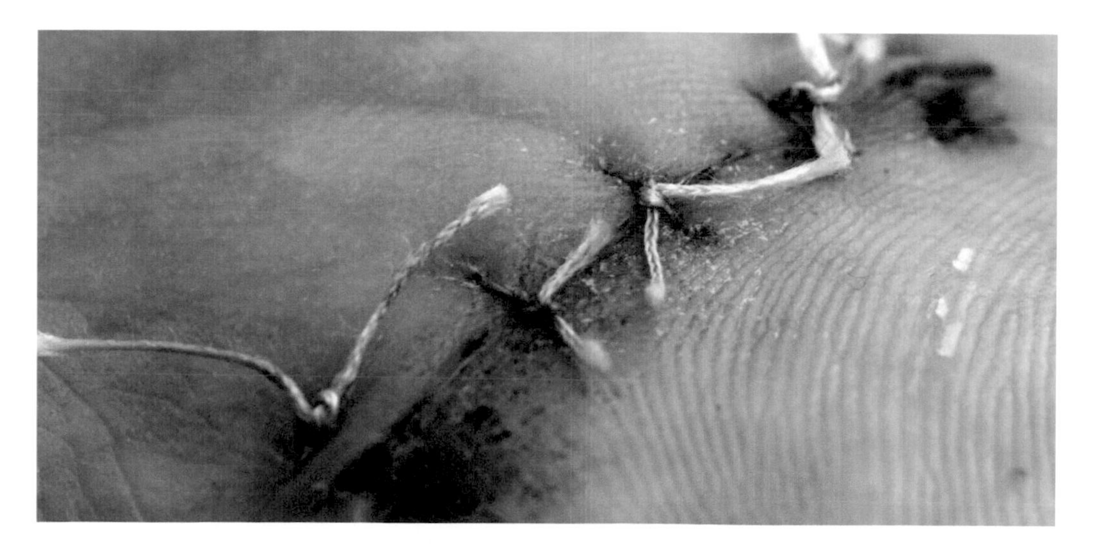

Dissolvable stitches are good for repairing muscles. Muscles need strong stitches at first. But they heal quickly.

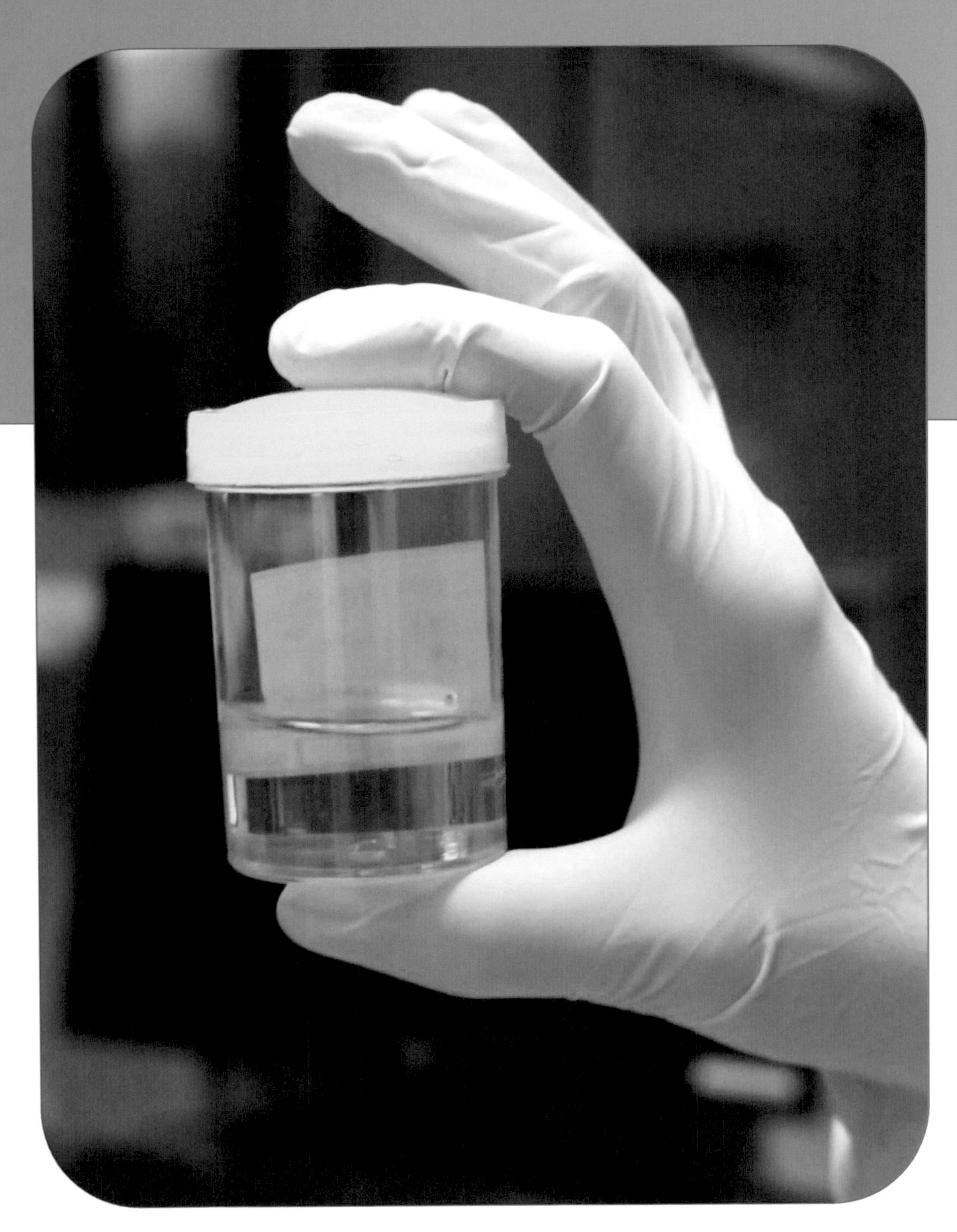

The color of your pee will depend on how much water you drink! The less water you drink, the darker your pee will be.

CHAPTER 3

PEE TESTING

Did you know your pee says a lot about you? It has traveled through your body. It gives clues about your body. This includes food, medicine, and germs.

Kidneys produce **urine**. Urine is another word for pee. Kidneys clean waste from your blood. The waste becomes urine. Urine is the body's way of getting rid of liquid waste. Without kidneys, poisons would build up. This would make us sick. Urine has more than 3,000 **compounds**. Compounds are things formed by combining 2 or more substances. These include water, salts, and chemicals.

Your urine gives your doctor information. Your doctor may ask for a urine test. They check to see if your kidneys are working. They check for signs of diseases. They check to see what's been in your body.

People pee in cups. These are **samples**. Samples are small bits of a whole. Doctors look at these samples. They check the color. They check to see if it's cloudy. Your urine should be light yellow and clear.

Doctors look at urine under a **microscope**. Microscopes are tools. They make small things look bigger. Doctors look at cells. They look to make sure germs aren't there. They make sure there aren't that many **crystals**. Crystals are small, rocklike formations.

Dipsticks are thin plastic sticks. They have special chemicals on them. They're dipped in urine. The dipstick chemicals react with the urine. They change color if something is wrong.

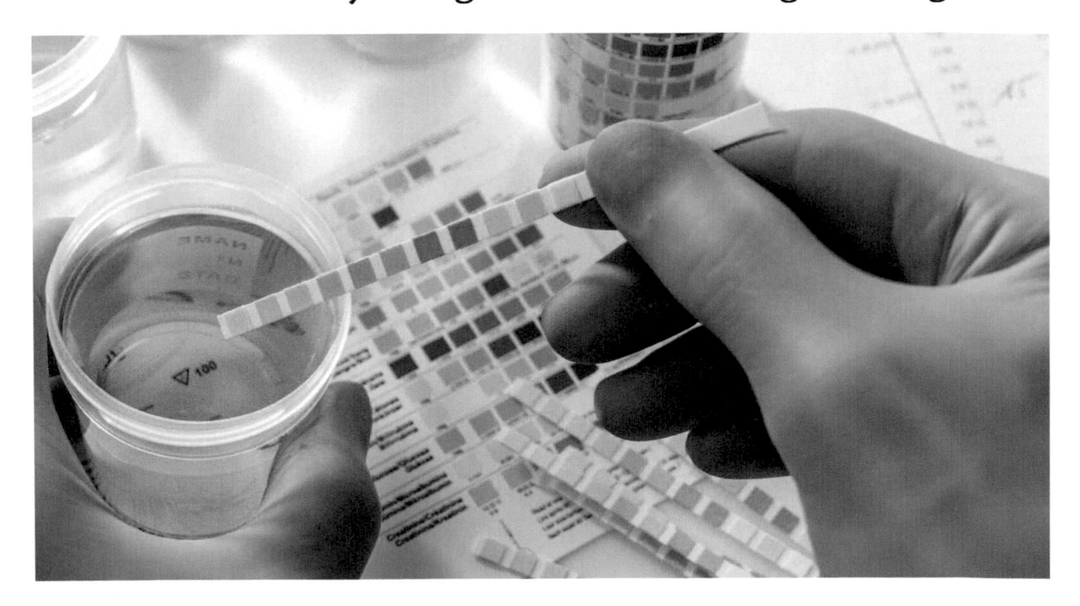

A person makes 6.3 cups (1.5 liters) of pee a day.

UNSOLVED MYSTERY

Mermaids are mythical creatures. They're human from the waist up. They don't have legs. They have fish tails instead. Sirenomelia is also known as Mermaid Syndrome. It's when babies are born with joined legs. They look like mermaids. They may or may not have feet. If they have feet, their feet look like flippers. They have other problems. Their organs and lungs may be damaged. They don't live long. No one knows what causes this. It's a medical mystery. Babies born with sirenomelia are very rare. It happens in 1 out of 100,000 births. This means scientists have a small sample to study. Babies born with sirenomelia are random. There is no pattern. This means scientists can't figure out what they have in common. They can't explain why it happens. They don't know much about it. This means they can't treat it.

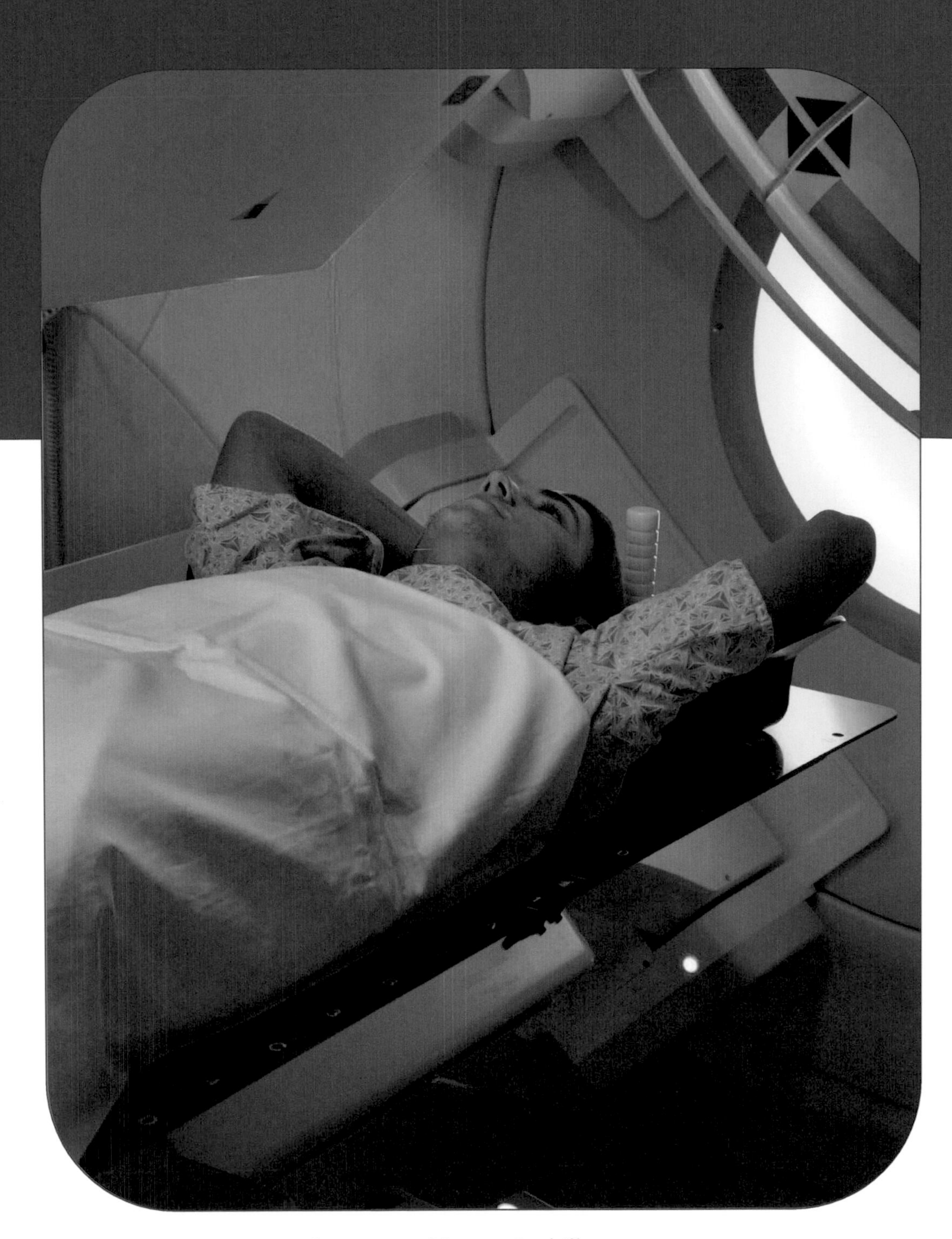

Doctors sometimes use X-rays to kill poisonous growths in bodies.

CHAPTER 4

X-RAY MACHINES

Have you ever had an **X-ray** done? X-rays are a form of **radiation**. Radiation is energy. It comes from a source. It travels through space. It can go through many materials.

X-rays are powerful waves of energy. They can go through things that light cannot. Doctors use X-ray machines. X-ray machines are tools. They take pictures of the inside of bodies. They take pictures of bones. They take pictures of muscles. They take pictures of air in lungs. Doctors can see diseases. They can see infections.

X-rays can damage the body's cells. Most doctors provide people with special blankets. This keeps them from getting too much radiation.

TEST IT OUT!

Washing hands keeps us healthy. People should wash their hand for 20 seconds. They should wash before eating. They should wash after touching things. Learn more about the power of washing hands.

Materials

- Pepper
- Bowl
- Water
- Dish soap

1. Sprinkle pepper into a bowl of water. Watch the pepper on top of the water. Water molecules cling together. Molecules are small units of a substance. Water molecule bonds create surface tension. This tension doesn't allow the pepper to mix in. That's why it floats.
2. Dip your finger in the bowl. See how the pepper sticks to your finger. This is like how germs stick to you.
3. Clean your finger. Then, cover it with dish soap. Dip it in the bowl.
4. Watch carefully. The pepper will scatter. It'll move to the edge of the bowl. It happens quickly. This shows how soap makes germs scatter. When added to water, soap breaks the water's surface tension. Water molecules pull away. This pulls off germs and dirt.

X-ray machines use a small amount of radiation. They make X-rays. They have a special tube to direct X-rays at a person. The X-rays pass through skin. They pass through muscles. Bones absorb the radiation.

There's a metal film behind the body. X-rays reach the body. They hit the film. X-ray machines are like cameras. Instead of light, they use X-rays. Pictures form based on which areas were exposed to the X-rays. Black areas are where X-rays passed through. These are soft parts like muscles. White areas are where X-rays were absorbed. These are hard parts like bones.

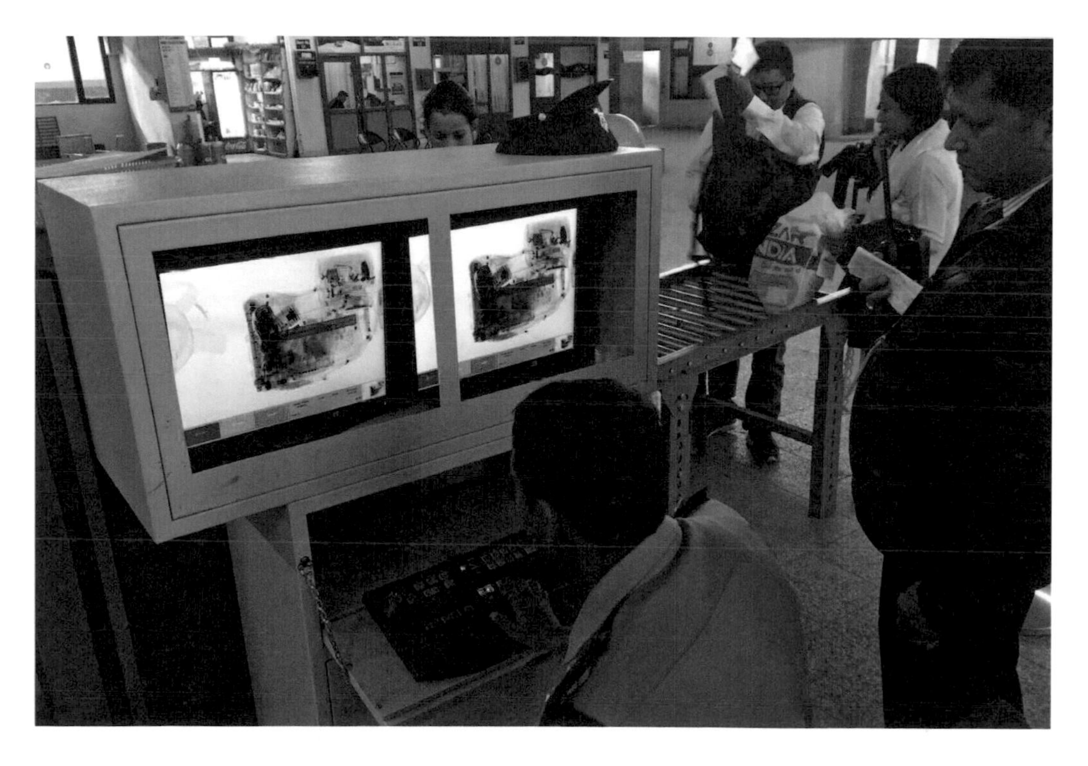

Airports use X-rays to look for hidden weapons in suitcases.

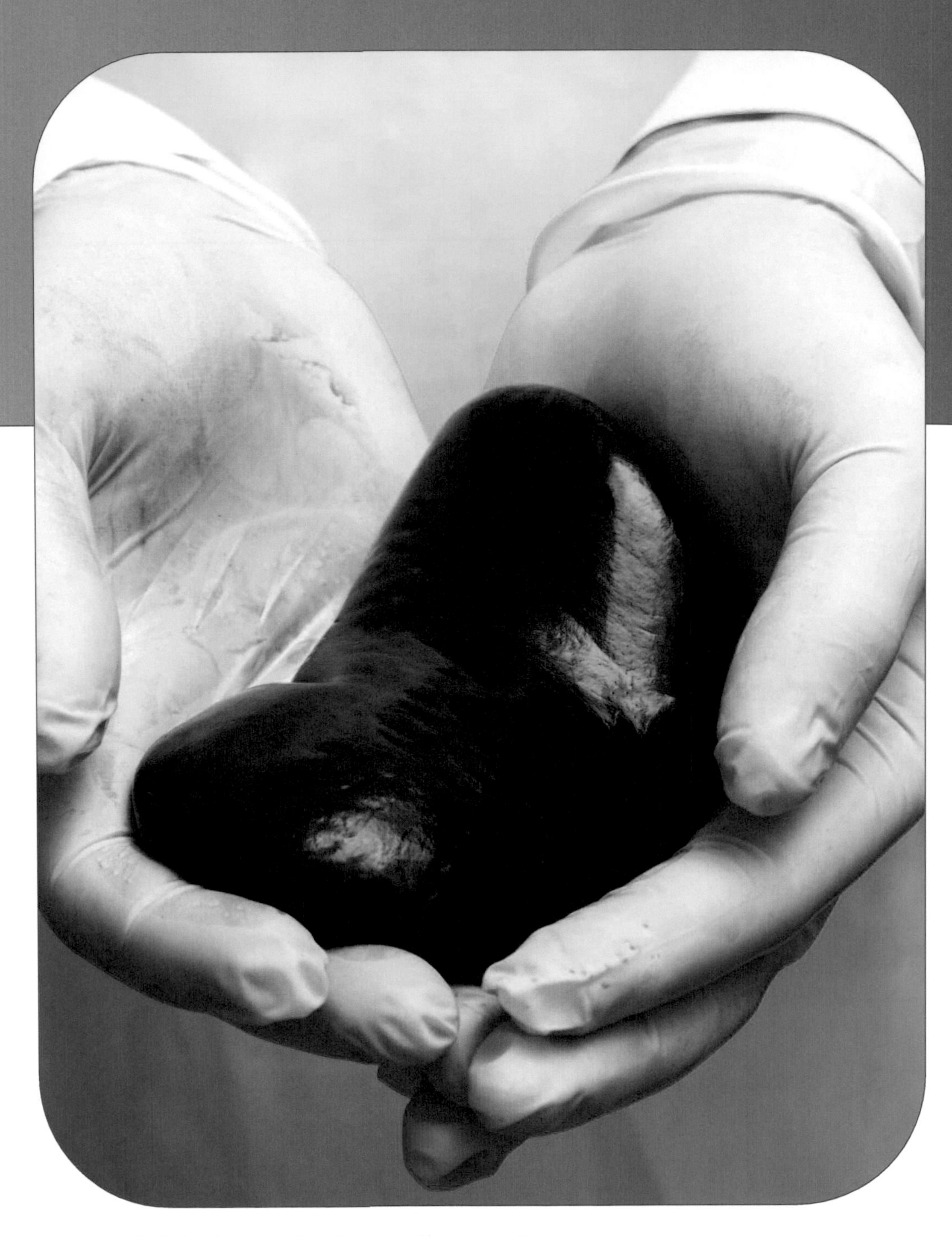

Kidney transplants are the most common.

CHAPTER 5

ORGAN TRANSPLANTS

Do you know anyone who's gotten an organ **transplant**? Transplant means to move or transfer. Human bodies have many organs. Examples are kidneys, hearts, and livers.

Some people have damaged organs. They need organ transplants. People donate their organs. They do this to help keep others alive. Doctors remove healthy organs from a body. They put it into another person's body. They hope the bodies don't reject the organs.

Organ transplants are hard. The organs need to be a good fit. They must be the same blood type and size.

SCIENTIST SPOTLIGHT

Julian Rios Cantu is from Mexico. He's a young inventor. At age 13, his mother got breast cancer. He watched her tumor get bigger. Tumors are dangerous growths. Cantu's mother had surgery to remove both her breasts. This inspired Cantu. Cantu wants to protect others from cancer. At age 18, he and his friend Antonio Torres formed a company called Higia Technologies. Cantu created a tool. The tool detects early signs of breast cancer. It's placed in women's bras. It needs to be worn for 1 hour every week. It has sensors that look for changes in body heat. Data is sent to the company's computers. Then, computer programs figure out the cancer risks. Cantu still needs to test this tool. He needs to raise money to make it. He's working on other medical inventions. An example is men's underwear that detects cancer.

Donated organs are recovered from bodies. They need to be shipped quickly. Organs can live outside of bodies for about 4 to 36 hours.

Donated organs are put in a cooler of ice. But cold organ cells don't work well. This would damage the organs. Organs need to be protected from extreme cold. They're flushed with special **solutions**. Solutions are liquid mixtures. They keep the organs' levels in check. They help keep organ cells alive. The cooler stores the organs and the solutions.

Keeping organs cool also slows down its energy. Their cells won't break down. They stay healthy.

Another way to store organs is by using a machine that pumps in living cells. But this costs a lot more than coolers.

It's unusual to dissect the face, arms, hands, or legs.

AUTOPSIES

Why did someone die? An **autopsy** is a detailed **dissection** of a dead person. Dissect means to cut open and examine. Autopsies are done to learn causes of death. Certain doctors do autopsies. They study diseases. They take lots of notes.

First, doctors examine the outside of the body. They weigh and measure the body. They look for marks. They look for injuries. They take hair and nail samples.

Second, doctors examine the inside of the body. They cut open the chest, stomach, and brain. These cuts don't form a lot of blood. Without a beating heart, blood doesn't bleed out of the body.

Autopsies were done in ancient times.

Third, doctors remove the ribs. They examine the organs. They look at the organs inside the body. Then, they remove the organs. They weigh the organs. They place the organs in solutions. The solutions keep organs from rotting. Each organ can be dissected.

Fourth, doctors take samples. They take blood samples. They take tissue samples. They take samples of food still in the stomach. Samples are sent to labs. They're tested.

Last, doctors put the body back together. They line the inside of the body with cotton. They sew it back up. For burials, they return organs to the bodies.

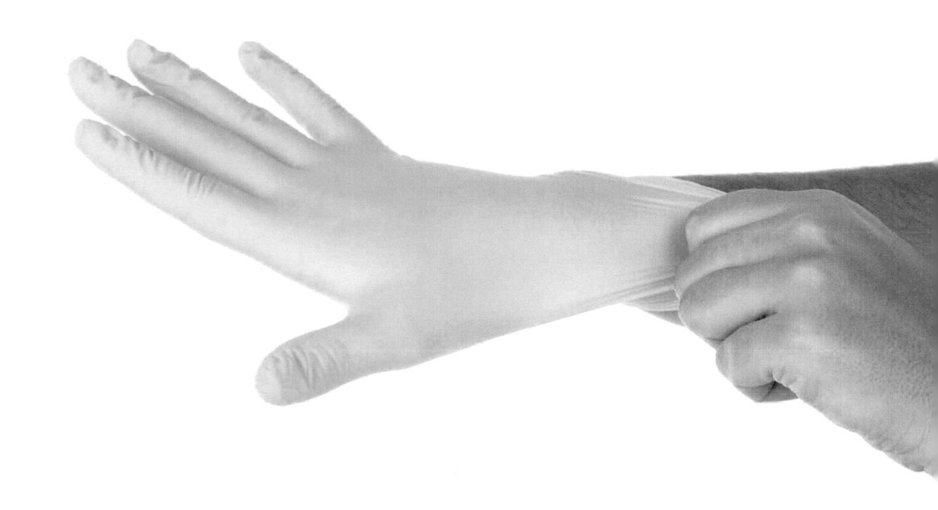

GLOSSARY

antibodies (AN-ti-bod-ees) substances produced by cells in the body that fight off sicknesses

autopsy (AW-top-see) a detailed dissection of a dead person

compounds (KOM-powndz) things formed by combining two or more substances

crystals (KRISS-tuhls) small, rocklike formations

decompose (dee-kuhm-POZE) to break down

dipsticks (DIP-stiks) thin plastic sticks with special chemicals used to test for diseases

diseases (duh-ZEEZ-ez) serious sicknesses

dissection (dih-SEKT-shun) the process of cutting

dissolves (dih-ZOLVZ) melts away

herd immunity (HURD i-MYOO-nuh-tee) resistance to the spread of diseases within a group of people

hosts (HOHSTS) people who carry diseases

immune (i-MYOON) resistant to sicknesses

microscope (MYE-kruh-skope) a tool used to see very small things

numb (NUHM) not feeling pain

outbreaks (OUT-brakes) sudden increases of infected people

radiation (RAY-dee-ay-shuhn) energy that travels through space and goes through many materials

samples (SAM-puhls) small amounts of something bigger used for testing

solutions (suh-LOO-shuhns) liquid mixtures

transplant (TRANSS-plant) to move or transfer

urine (YOOR-uhn) pee

vaccines (vak-SEENS) substances used to stimulate the production of antibodies to protect against diseases

X-ray (EKS-ray) a powerful wave of energy

LEARN MORE

Farndon, John, and Venita Dean (illus.). *Strange Medicine: A History of Medical Remedies*. Minneapolis, MN: Hungry Tomato, 2017.

Human Body! New York, NY: DK Publishing, 2017.

Loh-Hagan, Virginia. *Strange Medicine*. Ann Arbor, MI: Cherry Lake Publishing, 2018.

INDEX